Feelings Are...?

By Ymkje Wideman-van der Laan
Illustrated by Jennifer Lackgren

Copyright 2013 Ymkje Wideman-van der Laan
All rights reserved. Designed by Awexdesign
ISBN-10: 1482396955
ISBN-13: 978-1482396959

For Logan

One day, while playing at her place
I noticed water on Grandma's face.
Oh my, she didn't smile at me!
I was surprised, what could this be?

I touched a drop, right on her cheek.
I asked her if there was a leak.
She laughed and said it was a tear,
Because there'd been sad news to hear.

She told me tears are the way we show
That we are sad, and helps others know
That we are very likely dealing
With something that has hurt our feelings.

I looked at her puzzled, my mouth ajar,
And asked her, "Grandma, feelings are...?"
My grandma hugged me, put me at ease,
And told me about...

The Feelings ABCs

A is for angry. That's how you feel when someone hurts you, or when they steal. Stealing is taking things and toys that belong to other girls and boys.

B

is for baffled. That is being surprised, like on a day that your schedule revised. Now why, oh why, did your day not go the way you expected it to flow?

C is for confused. That's when nothing makes sense, and you are starting to feel quite tense. But don't you worry, things will work out, once you understand what it's all about.

D is for depressed. That's a very sad feeling when with big problems you are dealing. When you feel like that, please talk it out, and tell someone what you're sad about.

E is for excited. That's when you know today on a trip to the zoo you will go. Doing fun things is very exciting, and something you can later put into writing.

F is for fulfilled. That's feeling content when you've completed a task to the end. That feels pretty good, don't you agree? Let's try that again, so fulfilled you will be.

G is for glad. You're glad when you've won a prize for something good you have done. Maybe it was for good grades on a test, or simply for doing your very best.

H is for happy. That's similar to glad, but even better than the glad feeling you had when you won a prize or passed a test. Feeling happy is more, and simply the best!

I is for indifferent. That means you don't care about things that are happening here or there. You're busy with things that matter to you, and don't really mind what others will do.

J is for jealous. Are you turning green? You are upset and you feel it is mean that others have something you wish you had. It makes you feel awful and very bad.

K is for keen. You are eager to do something that has been required of you. You are raring to go, and jump out of your seat to work on a task until it's complete.

L is for loved. That's the warm fuzzy glow that you always get when you certainly know your family will do whatever it takes to love and protect you, no matter the stakes.

M is for miserable. That's a big word for a feeling worse than you ever have heard. Sometimes when you're sick, that's how you will feel until you're all better, and were able to heal.

N is for nervous. When you do something new, you're nervous and frantic about missing your cue. Hey, you can do it. Don't lose any sleep. You will feel better if you breathe really deep.

O is for optimistic. That's when you look at the bright side of any problem or crook. You firmly believe that not everything's bad, and that there is always some good to be had.

P is for proud. That's what you are when you do something well and deserve a star. You feel very good and you'll get a high five. You're being successful, and on that you will thrive.

Q is for quizzical. That's when you wonder, "Whatever that means!" or "What does that fall under?" You think and you think, but you don't understand. "This is too hard, this is way out of hand."

R is for rejected. That's what you feel when you hear a friend say, "I don't really like you, I don't want you to play." Feeling rejected is not nice at all. Let's include others now, and remember, don't stall!

I don't want you to play!

S is for suspicious.

That's when you suspect that what someone told you is incorrect. You just have that feeling that something is wrong, and want to discover the truth before long.

T is for tired. You know what that is. It's what you feel after a long day of biz. You've been running and jumping until you were steaming, so you're ready for bed and a good night of dreaming.

U is for unloved. Now that's very sad, because no one should ever feel that bad. Love is important! Let's take off that "un," so we'll all feel loved when the day is done.

V is for vengeful. That's a nasty emotion we should not give into, not even a notion. It means that you're hurt and want to hurt back, but that's never the answer, you're on the wrong track.

W is for worried. Are things working out? You are not so sure, and you're starting to doubt. When you feel worried, say what's bothering you, so someone can give you a different view.

You can do it!

X is for xenophobic. Now that's a strange word. In fact, it is stranger than I've ever heard. It means you're afraid of strange people, just very scared. Now aren't those much easier words, when compared?

Y is for yearning. That's when you want to do something special, like eat a croissant. You know it is baking, you can hardly wait for it to be ready. It's going to taste great!

Z is for zealous.

You really can't wait to learn all about feelings, like love, fear, and hate. You are raring to go, that's the meaning of zealous, which is something that can make others jealous.

Now that you have learned all of these ABCs,
How are you feeling, a bit more at ease?
I hope that this story explained a bit more
About what all these different feelings are for.

Of course, there are many more feelings than this.
If you learn these to start, you are a real whiz.
Knowing what you and others are feeling
Will help keep your world from rocking and reeling.

Logan drew 10 little red dogs   and hid them in the pages of this book. Can you find them?

About the Author

Ymkje Wideman-van der Laan is a writer, editor, and proofreader. In 2006, she assumed the care of her 6-month old grandson, Logan. There were signs of autism at an early age, and the diagnosis became official in 2009. She has been his advocate, and passionate about promoting autism awareness ever since. Logan is the inspiration behind *Feelings Are...?* and other children's books she wrote for him. You can find out more about her and her books at www.ymkje.com and www.autism-is.com

Note to Parents and Caregivers

On one particularly difficult day, after receiving some sad news, my grandson saw me wipe away a tear. He touched my cheek and remarked matter-of-factly, "There is water on your cheek, Grandma. It leaks!"

Children with autism often do not sense the feelings of others, and can have difficulty recognizing or relating to abstract emotions. I wrote *Feelings Are…?* to help my grandson learn about emotions and respecting others' feelings. He loves ABCs and he caught on quickly. One of his favorites is "Y is for yearning." He sure loves those croissants!

Reviewing *The Feelings ABCs* often with my grandson was a great first step in helping him learn to recognize and respect the feelings of others more. I hope this book will be helpful to other children with autism also.

The Author

26389651R00024

Printed in Great Britain
by Amazon